Tigers

Laura Marsh

NATIONAL GEOGRAPHIC

Washington, D.C.

For Claire and Ellie
—L. F. M.

Design by YAY! Design

Library of Congress Cataloging-in-Publication Data
Marsh, Laura F.
National Geographic readers. Tigers / by Laura Marsh. —1st ed.
p. cm.
ISBN 978-1-4263-0911-3 (pbk. : alk. paper) — ISBN 978-1-4263-0912-0 (library binding : alk. paper)
1. Tiger. I. Title.
QL737.C23M2748 2012
599.756—dc23
2011035282

Cover, Gerry Ellis/Minden Pictures; 1, Martin Harvey/Corbis; 2, Eric Isselée/Shutterstock; 4, Ron Kimball/Kimball Stock; 6 (top), DLILLC/Corbis; 6 (bottom), Terry Whittaker/FLPA; 7, Tom and Pat Leeson/Kimball Stock; 8 (top), Michael Nichols/NationalGeographicStock.com; 8 (center), Andyworks/iStockphoto.com; 8 (bottom), Mike Liu/iStockphoto.com; 9 (top), Matthew Cole/iStockphoto.com; 9 (top, center), Daniel Cox/Photolibrary RM/Getty Images; 9 (bottom, center), Fuse/Getty Images; 9 (bottom), Dimitar Marinov/iStockphoto.com; 10, Wild Bill Melton/Corbis; 11, Anup Shah/naturepl.com; 13, Digital Vision/Getty Images; 14 (top), PhotoDisc; 14 (center), Dirk Freder/iStockphoto.com; 14 (bottom), Jens Klingebiel/iStockphoto.com; 15, (top, left), Michael Nichols/NationalGeographicStock.com; 15 (top, right), Schalke fotografie/Melissa Schalke/Shutterstock; 15 (bottom, left), Michael Nichols/NationalGeographicStock.com; 15 (bottom, right), Tiago Estima/iStockphoto.com; 16, Eric Isselée/Shutterstock; 17, Ocean/Corbis; 18 (top), Ocean/Corbis; 18 (bottom), Michael Nichols/NationalGeographicStock.com; 19, Renee Lynn/Corbis; 20, Steve Bloom Images/Alamy; 21 (top), DLILLC/Corbis; 21 (bottom), Lynn M. Stone/naturepl.com; 22-23, Gerry Ellis/Minden Pictures; 27, Savigny/npl/Minden Pictures; 28, Terry Whittaker/Frank Lane Picture Agency/Corbis; 30 (top), Digital Vision; 30 (center), Ingo Arndt/Minden Pictures; 30 (bottom), Suzan Charnock/iStockphoto.com; 31 (top left), Michael Nichols/NationalGeographicStock.com; 31 (top right), Martin Ruegner/Getty Images; 31 (bottom, left), drbimages/iStockphoto.com; 31 (bottom, right), M. Robbemont/Shutterstock; 32 (top, left), Michael Nichols/NationalGeographicStock.com; 32 (top, right), Gerry Ellis/Minden Pictures; 32 (left, center), Franco Tempesta; 32 (right, center), Galyna Andrushko/Shutterstock; 32 (bottom, left), Schafer & Hill/Getty Images; 32 (bottom, right), Theo Allofs/Minden Pictures/NationalGeographicStock.com.

Printed in the United States of America
11/WOR/1

Table of Contents

PURR-fectly Big Cats

Bengal Tiger

Tigers are big and beautiful animals. They are strong and powerful, too. Tigers are the biggest cats in the world.

A Tiger's Home

Tigers live in the forest. They spend a lot of time in the water, too. They live in hot places like Indonesia. They live in cold places like Russia.

Indochinese Tiger

Siberian Tiger

Tigers that live in cold places are bigger than other tigers. They also have thicker fur to keep them warm.

Built for Hunting

Tigers are fierce hunters. Their bodies are built for catching prey.

Coat

A tiger's stripes camouflage it in tall grass and dry leaves. Its prey may not see the tiger until it's too late.

Teeth

Four large teeth help tigers kill prey quickly.

Eyes

A tiger's terrific eyesight helps it hunt at night.

Paws

Big paws with soft pads help a tiger walk quietly. Sharp claws hook into prey and don't let go.

Tail

A long tail helps a tiger keep its balance when moving quickly.

Back legs

Big muscles help a tiger dash or leap at its prey.

Tiger Term

CAMOUFLAGE: An animal's natural color or form that blends in with what is around it

PREY: An animal that is eaten by another animal

Meat Eater

Tigers are carnivores, animals that eat meat. Their favorite foods are large, hooved animals such as buffalo, deer, and wild pigs.

A hungry tiger can chow down 80 pounds of meat in one meal. That's about 320 hamburgers!

Tiger Turf

Besides hunting, tigers spend a lot of time marking their territory. They are not good at sharing!

Tigers make long scratch marks on trees. They also rub their faces on trees and leave smelly scents. This tells other tigers to stay away.

Tiger Term

TERRITORY: An area that an animal protects from other animals

Siberian Tiger

Cool Cat Facts

Check out
these neat facts
about tigers.

No two tigers have
exactly the same
stripes.

Whiskers help a tiger feel its
way in the dark.

Large paws keep
Siberian tigers from
sinking in deep snow.

Tigers can live in temperatures as low as -40 degrees Fahrenheit.

Tigers are great swimmers. They are never far from water.

A tiger's front teeth are three inches long.

Tigers have much better hearing than humans.

Cubs

A female tiger usually has two or
three cubs at one time. The cubs
weigh about four pounds at birth.

The mother raises the cubs
by herself. Male and female tigers
come together only to have cubs.
Otherwise, adult tigers live alone.

Bengal Tiger

A mother Bengal tiger nurses her young.

The cubs drink their mother's milk. After three or four months, they start to eat meat.

Tiger cubs play games. They chase, leap, and pounce. They are learning how to be good hunters. When they are two years old, young tigers leave their family to find their own territories.

Tiger Talents

Tigers are full-grown when they leave their families. They are big, heavy cats, but they can climb trees and jump great distances.

Bengal Tiger

In fact, tigers can leap as far as 30 feet. That's as long as five adult men lying head to toe!

And, unlike house cats, tigers are good swimmers. They like to cool off in rivers and pools.

Sumatran Tiger

The White Tiger

The white Bengal tiger is very rare. It can't grow orange fur. Its white coat, brown stripes, and icy blue eyes are quite a sight.

You won't find a white Bengal tiger in the wild. But you might be able to see one in a zoo.

Q What's striped and bouncy?

A A tiger on a pogo stick!

White Bengal Tiger

Tigers in Trouble

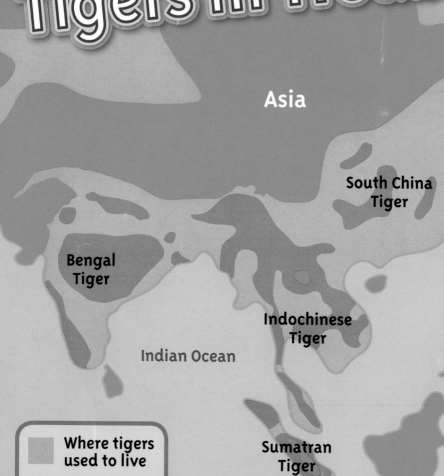

Asia

South China Tiger

Bengal Tiger

Indochinese Tiger

Indian Ocean

Sumatran Tiger

Where tigers used to live
Where tigers live today

Tigers are endangered. About 100 years ago, there were 100,000 tigers in the wild. Today there are less than 3,500.

**Siberian
Tiger**

Pacific Ocean

There are five different kinds of tigers today. They are the Bengal (BEN-gol), South China, Indochinese (in-doh-chi-NEEZ), Sumatran (soo-MAH-truhn), and Siberian (si-BEER-ee-uhn) tiger. Three other kinds of tigers have already become extinct.

Why are tigers disappearing?

Tigers are losing their habitat. People cut down trees. Tigers live and find food in the forests. When forests disappear, so do tigers.

People also kill tigers for their body parts. Their skins are used for rugs. Other parts are used to make traditional Chinese medicines.

Killing tigers is against the law. But it still happens today.

Tiger Term

HABITAT: The place where a plant or animal naturally lives

Q What do you get when you cross a tiger with a snowman?

A Frostbite!

South China Tiger

27

Helping Tigers

Bengal Tiger

Though tigers are in trouble, there is good news. New forest areas for tigers have been found. Also, people are planting trees where forests have been cut down.

You can help, too. Tell your family and friends about what you've learned. We can all work together to keep tigers on our planet!

Stump Your Parents

Can your parents answer these questions about tigers? You might know more than they do!

Answers at bottom of page 31.

How do tigers spend their time?

A. Howling
B. Hunting and marking their territory
C. Sharing their territory
D. Eating plants

What is special about a tiger's paws?

A. They are small but powerful
B. They don't sink in deep snow
C. They have three toes
D. They make noise when walking

How do tigers live?

A. Alone, except when a mother is raising her young
B. In groups of three to four
C. In groups of five to eight
D. With all their friends

What's important about a tiger's striped coat?

A. It sticks out
B. Its pattern is the same as other tigers'
C. It comes in many colors
D. It camouflages the tiger

What do tigers like to eat?

A. Fruits and berries
B. Insects
C. Meat — and lots of it!
D. People

Where do tigers like to live?

A. In the desert
B. Near water
C. In the mountains
D. On the savanna

What is a baby tiger called?

A. A pup
B. A kit
C. A cub
D. A gosling

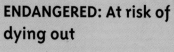

CAMOUFLAGE: An animal's natural color or form that blends in with what is around it

ENDANGERED: At risk of dying out

EXTINCT: A group of animals no longer living

HABITAT: The place where a plant or animal naturally lives

PREY: An animal that is eaten by another animal

TERRITORY: An area that an animal protects from other animals